Original title:
Tidings of Comfort and Joy

Copyright © 2024 Creative Arts Management OÜ
All rights reserved.

Author: Alec Davenport
ISBN HARDBACK: 978-9916-94-060-0
ISBN PAPERBACK: 978-9916-94-061-7

The Light That Guides Us Home

In socks that slip and slide, we creep,
By twinkling lights, we never sleep.
Chasing shadows, making noise,
Festive fun, our silly joys.

With cookies stacked as tall as me,
And laughter loud as the TV.
A candle's glow, a wink or two,
We fumble forth, a merry crew.

The Gift of Open Arms

In a bear hug that's way too tight,
We bounce around like kites in flight.
With playful jabs and silly cheer,
Embraces full of love, my dear.

Like spaghetti tossed in the air,
We share the joy without a care.
Each hug a present, warm and bright,
Wrapped in giggles, pure delight.

A Haven Found in Togetherness

In a pile of snacks, we all reside,
Like sardines who've gone on a ride.
With faces smeared in cake and pie,
We laugh and snort, we can't deny.

A blanket fortress, pillows galore,
We plot and scheme to snack some more.
A patchwork quilt of quirky quirks,
In silliness, the magic lurks.

The Warmth of Beneath the Branches

Amidst the tinsel, we giggle and sway,
As ornaments try to roll away.
Under branches soft and wide,
We sip our cocoa, cheeks applied.

With boots on feet, and hats askew,
We dance around like cows in stew.
Beneath the boughs, we let thoughts flow,
Finding laughter, soft and slow.

Lanterns of Collective Heart

Lanterns glow like smiley faces,
Bringing warmth to all our spaces.
With popcorn flying here and there,
We laugh till milk comes out our hair.

Jingle bells and clumsy dance,
Tripping on our silly chance.
The dog steals snacks with quick delight,
As we embrace this joyful night.

Chasing Stars of Togetherness

We chase the stars, but trip on shoes,
Bouncing laughter all around in blues.
Chasing dreams and silly schemes,
Even the cat joins in our memes.

Falling snow brings frosty cheer,
As we roll jokes and tasty beer.
Oh, what fun in this crazy game,
Together we'll never be the same.

Nurtured by Memories

Nurtured by laughter, we share a plate,
Old stories tell our twisted fate.
Grandma's cookies, slightly burnt,
But who would care? Our hearts are learned.

Each memory wrapped in silly threads,
We recall the times when we fell on heads.
With giggles bouncing off the walls,
Echoing through these cherished halls.

The Beauty of Reunion

Reunions bring our quirks to blend,
With hugs and jokes that never end.
Mismatched sweaters, silly ties,
Laughter echoes, reaching the skies.

As we toast to awkward moments past,
In friendship's glow, we're unsurpassed.
With each new laugh, we further mend,
The beautiful chaos that we defend.

Whispers of Warmth

There's a cat on a chair, he thinks he's the king,
Sipping hot cocoa, he makes my heart sing.
With a sock on his paw, he leaps without care,
It's a royal decree, no room left to spare.

The dog tries to dance, but he trips on a shoe,
His tail wags with glee, as if he just knew.
A squirrel in the window shares secrets with me,
Their chatter and giggles, the best company.

The Glow of Solace

In the fridge sits a pie, it's meant for the feast,
Yet I'm eyeing the snacks, I'm snack-obsessed beast.
With cheese and some crackers, I plot my delight,
Caution thrown to the wind, it's a snacking night.

A snowman's my buddy, with a carrot for nose,
He steals all my scarves and he giggles, I suppose.
With each little flake, I laugh and I cheer,
Who knew winter could bring so much good cheer?

Embrace of Serenity

My neighbor's bright lights blink like they're lost,
They dance in the dark, at a very high cost.
But he laughs at my jokes, and we sip spiked cider,
Life's little joy, our nighttime glider.

With gingerbread men that have lost their way,
One's missing a button, but what can I say?
We bake with such laughter, it makes the day bright,
All thanks to a flour-covered, impish delight.

Radiant Threads of Hope

I once wore a sweater that itched like a bear,
Yet I boldly declared, for my friends, I would wear.
Through giggles and grumbles, we formed quite a crew,
Fashion police be warned, we don't care for you!

When life gets too serious, I tell them some jokes,
My delivery's awkward, but joy never chokes.
With each silly grin, our troubles take flight,
Laughter's the beacon that glows in the night.

Mosaic of Cherished Moments

In a world of quirky laughs, we play,
Stumbling through the joy of each day.
A dance with socks that do not match,
In this silly life, we find our catch.

Cookies burned, yet smiles remain,
Wacky stories that drive us insane.
Juggling dreams, we trip and fall,
Yet in each giggle, we stand tall.

A cat dressed up, thinks it's a queen,
Silly antics, oh how they glean.
Moments captured, framed in cheer,
Laughter bubbles, loud and clear.

From mishaps that are quite absurd,
To heartfelt jokes that go unheard.
We cherish moments, embrace the fun,
In this mosaic, we're all one.

Fields of Laughter

In fields where giggles grow so high,
We let our worries wave goodbye.
With every tumble and silly chase,
Laughter blooms, fills up the space.

Tripping over garden gnomes,
We laugh as if we're all at home.
The grass stains tell the tales we weave,
Of joyful hearts, and tricks up our sleeve.

A puppy somersaults, unaware,
Sending giggles into the air.
With each snort, we raise our cheers,
In this field, there's no room for fears.

Picnics turned into food fights,
We laugh 'til we forget the nights.
In laughter's embrace, we all rejoice,
In fields of humor, we find our voice.

A Tapestry of Kindness

Stitches of laughter, woven to share,
With every mishap, we show we care.
A kind word wrapped in a funny twist,
In this tapestry, nothing's missed.

The neighbor's cat steals our lunch,
Yet we all giggle at the munch.
Generosity in our silly ways,
Kindness grows through laughter's rays.

When life throws pies, we take a bite,
Fluffy cream can make things right.
With goofy socks and wild hairdos,
We share kindness in the things we choose.

In every tickle and playful jest,
We find the love that we cherish best.
A tapestry bright with colors bold,
In laughter and kindness, our hearts unfold.

The Hearth's Gentle Embrace

In a room filled with snacks,
The chair squeaks with glee,
Grandpa's snoring, what a racket,
His dreams play hide and seek.

The cat steals the turkey,
While the dog steals a roll,
Laughter mingles with chaos,
What a comical goal!

Cousins chase around,
Dressed in mismatched socks,
We aim for the jelly,
And dodge the flying rocks.

With cocoa and laughter,
We toast to the day,
Here's to blunders and mishaps,
In our funny ballet!

A Journey to Tranquil Shores

We set sail on a rubber duck,
With paddles made of spoons,
The captain's got a goofy grin,
As we dodge the beachball moons.

Flip-flops are our anchors,
As we navigate with flair,
Sunscreen in our eyes,
And no one's got a care.

Seagulls snatch our sandwiches,
With stealthy swoops and dives,
But laughter rules our ocean,
As we barely survive.

Underneath the sun's embrace,
We sing off-key, rejoice,
Here's to mixing up the waves,
With laughter as our choice!

Moments Wrapped in Contentment

On a couch piled high with snacks,
We watch the show, half awake,
Popcorn flies and giggles bloom,
As we fix our silly mistakes.

Uncles tell their wild tales,
Of sledding down a hill,
Each twist brings endless laughter,
And the stories never still.

A napkin fight ignites the room,
With crumpled paper balls,
We roll around in fits of giggles,
As hilarity enthralls.

As night falls soft and gentle,
We're wrapped in warmth, not strife,
These moments shared together,
Make the funniest life!

The Dance of Grateful Hearts

We gather round the table,
Each chair a throne of cheer,
With mashed potatoes flying high,
And laughter ringing clear.

Grandma's wig flies off her head,
As she twirls in delight,
We dance around the kitchen,
In our colorful socks tonight.

A toast made with orange juice,
In mismatched plastic cups,
We giggle for the silly things,
That lead to joyful hiccups.

With every step, our hearts entwine,
In this festival of joy,
For love's the greatest punchline,
In life's great, goofy ploy!

Garden of Lasting Smiles

In a garden where the giggles grow,
Laughter sprouts like flowers in a row.
With every joke that tickles the air,
Even the gnomes can't help but stare.

Butterflies dance to the punny tunes,
Bees buzzing jokes like buzzing cartoons.
Squirrels chuckle as they gather their nuts,
While rabbits roll in their playful ruts.

Hearthside Conversations

Gather 'round, let the banter flow,
With marshmallows ready for a cheeky show.
Tales of socks that vanish in the night,
And cookies that mysteriously take flight.

Comfy chairs wiggle with every roguish jest,
While the cat plots mischief, doing its best.
As hot cocoa spills, we erupt into glee,
Who knew winter chats could be so zany?

Timeless Threads of Unity

With every stitch, a giggle is sewn,
In this quirky quilt of love we've grown.
With mismatched colors and patterns askew,
Even the fabric gives a chuckle or two.

Stitches like secrets weave us together,
We promise to laugh, no matter the weather.
In the tapestry of moments we share,
We'll always wear smiles—beyond compare!

Horizon of Goodwill

On this horizon where cheer multiplies,
Even the sun gives a wink from the skies.
With jokes like sunbeams, laughter soars,
The moon joins in, tapping its metaphorical floors.

From hilltops to valleys where kindness abounds,
A parade of chuckles fills all the sounds.
As we skip through this world, hand in hand,
Spreading joy like confetti across the land.

A Symphony of Restful Days

In pajamas I dance, feeling quite bold,
With popcorn and laughter, the stories unfold.
Chasing the cat, who steals the last slice,
In this silly chaos, my heart feels so nice.

Binges of shows, the remote is my throne,
As the dog snores loudly, I'm never alone.
With snacks piled high, the joy feels so wild,
Each moment we share makes me feel like a child.

The couch is my kingdom on this lazy spree,
In my fortress of pillows, I'm utterly free.
Even the plants seem to giggle along,
In this symphony of rest, we are all where we belong.

The Caress of Peaceful Evenings

When the sun takes its bow and the stars start to peek,
A warm cup of cocoa is what I now seek.
With slippers like clouds, I shuffle about,
In the glow of the lamp, there's no room for doubt.

A snack-wielding squirrel is my only guest,
He steals all the snacks—oh, what a bold jest!
With laughter and chuckles, the evening does hum,
Together we share in this warm, silly drum.

As the moon tells its tales in the wink of the night,
I whisper my dreams to its soft, silver light.
With a giggle at shadows that dance on the wall,
Peace wraps around me, a comforting shawl.

Gentle Echoes of Affection

In the kitchen we bumble, flour coats our nose,
With giggles and chuckles, that's just how it goes.
Cookies go flying, and frosting's a fight,
But oh, what a joy when the chaos feels right.

I love how you snort when you laugh just too loud,
As we spin through the kitchen like a clumsy cloud.
Every sweet moment is wrapped up in glee,
Echoes of joy are the best company.

The cat watches closely, a judge in disguise,
As we mix up the batter with gleaming bright eyes.
Silly as ever, our hearts feel so bold,
In the gentle affection, our love, pure as gold.

A Tapestry of Shared Dreams

With crayons and paper we splash colors bright,
Drawing our dreams in the soft morning light.
A monster from Venus eats pancakes with flair,
And a dragon named Gary will take us both there.

We giggle at worlds that we weirdly create,
Imagining lands where we're both very late.
In castles of marshmallows and lakes made of jam,
Our laughter's the magic, our hearts in a slam.

As bedtime approaches with yawns and delight,
I'll tuck you in tight and whisper goodnight.
Our tapestry woven with threads of our fun,
Each dream that we share is a new morning's sun.

The Truths We Hold Dear

We gather around, all cheery and bright,
With cookies and pies, what a wonderful sight!
Uncle Joe's jokes are a bit too insane,
Yet we all laugh, even through the pain.

The cat's on the table, oh what a mess,
A sprinkle of fur adds to each dish, no less!
A toast to those moments, a wink and a cheer,
For laughter's the secret we hold very dear.

Whispers of Warmth

Do you smell that? It's Aunt May's burnt pie,
It could take down a plane, oh my oh my!
Yet we bite in, every face is a grin,
For love in the kitchen is where it begins.

Grandpa's asleep, with his snore and his snooze,
Dreaming of steaks, or the last evening news.
We'll nudge him awake, with a wink and a cheer,
For smiles are the whispers that keep us all near.

Embracing the Light

The lights on the tree blink in a dance,
While cousin Tim stumbles, giving us a chance.
To laugh at his antics, so clumsy and spry,
He'll slip and he'll giggle, oh my, what a guy!

We pile on the couch, like a big furry quilt,
Sharing tales of the year that we've built.
With snacks in our laps and hearts that unite,
We savor these moments, alive with delight.

Serenade of the Heart

As the carolers sing with their off-pitch allure,
Sister Jane joins in, oh but that's quite the cure!
We all take a turn, showing voice wild and free,
It's so bad, yet we laugh, like a messy spree.

So let's raise a glass, to the mishaps and cheer,
To the memories made and the love that is near.
In this merry circus, where everyone's part,
We find every laugh is a song of the heart.

Reflections of Peace

In a world where socks get lost,
And laundry hangs at all the cost.
I sit with coffee, warm and bright,
Wishing laundry would take flight.

The cat thinks the sun is a throne,
Chasing rays, he's lost and alone.
I chuckle soft at his big plans,
As he pounces on sunbeams like fans.

Neighbors argue over trees,
While I giggle with this mild tease.
I'll trade my pie for a good laugh,
Come join me for a slice and a gaff.

In laughter's embrace we find peace,
With silly quirks, our joys increase.
So raise a toast with cheer and glee,
In quirky bliss, we all agree!

Savoring the Moments

With cookies burnt, a typical feat,
I smile and serve up a fine treat.
My dog eyes me, wagging away,
As if to say, 'I'll eat today!'

Each mishap becomes a small tale,
Like when the cat climbed up the rail.
We'll laugh till we can barely breathe,
In moments shared, we find reprieve.

Unruly prints from muddy shoes,
My heart chuckles at these ruse cues.
A treasure hunt in every mess,
Who knew chaos could be such a bless?

From spilled juice to rogue balloons,
We dance to our own silly tunes.
Savoring moments, sweet and bright,
We find our joy in the pure light.

Banners of Bliss

Banners flying high above,
Waving bright like a friendly dove.
Caught in cake and icing swirl,
Life's a party, watch it twirl!

A hamster named Sir Fluffypaws,
Chewing on confetti, he gives applause.
He rolls in circles, all around,
A fuzzy jester, joy unbound.

In the kitchen, chaos reigns,
Spaghetti dancing, oh the gains!
Laughter mixing with herbs and spice,
Cooking's a circus, oh how nice!

With funny hats and socks askew,
We gather 'round to share our brew.
In little joys, our spirits lift,
Celebrating life, our greatest gift!

A Journey to Contentment

In slippers worn and coffee spills,
I ride the waves of small life thrills.
Navigating through the snack parade,
With popcorn trails, my journey's laid.

The phone it rings, another joke,
A friend that knows just how to poke.
We share a laugh, our giggles soar,
In silly moments, who needs more?

With every stumble, each light-hearted fall,
The journey's mapped in laughter's call.
So let's embrace this fun-filled ride,
In joy and peace, we'll take our stride.

Through quirky paths together dance,
In mischief's light, we take our chance.
Contentment found in every jest,
With friends around, we are truly blessed!

Echoes of Cherished Laughter

In the kitchen, a pie takes flight,
A cat leaps up, it's quite a sight!
We giggle at flour on Dad's nose,
He looks like a ghost in bakery clothes.

Grandma's stories spin like yarn,
About a snail that drove a car,
We snicker at the tales she tells,
While sipping cocoa, ringing bells.

Beneath the Starry Canopy

Under stars that twinkle bright,
We dance around in warm moonlight.
A sock stuck high on the tree,
We laugh and shout, "That's a sight to see!"

Uncle Fred sings off-key with flair,
The dog howls back, in deep despair.
Though laughter echoes, slow and clear,
We might just lose our voice from cheer.

The Blanket of Kindness

A blanket made of hugs and threads,
Covers the couch where laughter spreads.
Friends drop in with silly hats,
And bring along their playful cats.

A riddle game with curious stunts,
How many are left when one more runs?
Chasing giggles all night long,
In this cozy home, we all belong.

Melodies of Heartfelt Reunion

When family gathers, joy takes flight,
We sing our songs through the night.
A cousin's joke turns into a play,
And now we all can't find our way.

With winks and nudges, we all conspire,
A pillow fight leads to silly fire.
In chaos, love wraps us tight,
Each chuckle glows, a guiding light.

A Chorus of Delight

In a land of merry sounds,
Laughter echoes all around.
Silly hats and jolly cheers,
Bring the joy that reappears.

Crispy cookies, milk in mugs,
Dance like happy, plump little bugs.
Puppies chasing their own tails,
It's a party where fun prevails.

Carols sung by out-of-tune,
Cats that howl at the full moon.
Prancing friends, they trip and fall,
Yet still they stand and have a ball.

As the snowflakes start to roam,
We find our way back home alone.
Wrapped in warmth, we share a grin,
For this is where the fun begins.

Harmony in Hibernation

Bears are snoring in their caves,
While squirrels plot their acorn saves.
Woolly socks and cozy sweaters,
Fuel our spirits in all weathers.

Laziness is the name of the game,
Catching naps without any shame.
Hot cocoa spills and goofy slips,
As winter grants us frosty trips.

Giggling geese on a frozen lake,
Waddle around, for goodness sake!
Snowmen sporting silly hats,
Dance with joy like silly cats.

In the deep of winter's night,
We'll share a laugh 'til morning light.
Hibernation? Quite the delight,
Let's nap away the chilly fright.

Seasons of Love's Return

When leaves turn gold and fall to ground,
We gather 'round to share what's found.
Pumpkin spice and candle glow,
Tell the tales of love, you know.

Friends with sweaters, holding hands,
Turkey feasts and clumsy bands.
Playing games, we laugh and cheer,
Hearts grow warm, the end is near.

Snowflakes dance like silly sprites,
Spreading joy on winter nights.
Mistletoe hung in awkward spots,
Oh how we love these funny knots.

With spring's warm kiss, the blooms arrive,
From cozy naps, we all revive.
Laughter's echo fills the air,
Love returns, and so does care.

Illuminated Paths

Streetlights twinkle like fairy lights,
As friends embark on silly flights.
Under the stars, they skip and hop,
A comedic tumble, and laughter won't stop.

Jolly hats and scarves that clash,
Sledding down the hill in a splash.
Muffins warm from the oven bright,
A secret stash shared just right.

Caking faces with snowy white,
Hot soup spills! What a funny sight.
In jovial chaos, we embrace,
The humor found in every case.

Through illuminated paths we roam,
Finding glee when far from home.
For laughter's glow is what we share,
In every moment, everywhere.

Gentle Embrace of the Soul

In winter's freeze, we wear our hats,
And sip on cocoa, with silly chats.
A snowball fight does start the night,
With giggles loud, what pure delight!

The cat is dressed, in reindeer style,
We laugh so hard, it's worth the while.
A jolly dance, both wild and free,
Our silly moves, a sight to see!

We build a man, from snowy fluff,
But somehow, he looks kind of tough.
With twigs for limbs and a carrot nose,
A funny sight, everybody knows!

As candles glow, we sing their tune,
With off-key notes, and giggles soon.
In this warm space, we feel so bold,
With laughter shared, our hearts unfold.

Twilight's Sweet Embrace

The twilight sky, a sassy show,
As stars appear, they start to glow.
With marshmallows stuck on a fork,
We roast them well, some tasty dork!

The fire crackles, flames jump high,
A squirrel joins in, oh my, oh my!
He steals our snacks, we laugh and cheer,
A little thief, we hold so dear!

We tell old tales with goofy flair,
Of ghosts and ghouls who float in air.
But in the end, we know it's light,
That fills our hearts this starry night!

As twilight fades to night so deep,
With dreams of laughter, we drift to sleep.
Together here, we feel so right,
A cozy bunch, what pure delight!

Lullabies of the Soul

The moonbeams dance on cozy beds,
With ticklish toes and sleepy heads.
A story time, we laugh and play,
With llamas in pajamas on display!

The stars above hum silly tunes,
Of dancing cats and flying balloons.
With snickers soft, we chase our fears,
While whispered tales bring merry cheers.

We sing our dreams with silly rhymes,
Of flying fish and silly climes.
A lullaby that makes us grin,
As sleepy eyes begin to spin!

In beds so warm, we snuggle tight,
And giggle softly 'til goodnight.
With love that wraps like a big hug,
Our hearts are full, all warm and snug.

The Glow of Togetherness

Gather 'round and pour the cheer,
With silly hats and snacks held near.
A game of charades starts to unfold,
With laughter bright and stories told!

The lights twinkle in jolly glee,
As Grandpa tries to dance with me.
A spin, a twirl, he takes a fall,
But laughs it off, he's having a ball!

The pie is burnt, but who cares wrong?
We munch away, as friends belong.
With crumbs that fall and plates held high,
In this sweet mess, we touch the sky!

So here we stand, all hand in hand,
In love and laughter, we make our stand.
Through ups and downs, we find our best,
In this warm glow, we are truly blessed!

Twilight Hues of Hope

As the sun takes its dive,
Squirrels prepare for their feast.
Chasing acorns like a drive,
Winter's silliness at least.

Frogs in hats hop about,
Dancing on snow, what a show!
Laughter spills from every shout,
As snowmen join in the flow.

The stars begin their bright winks,
While carolers misplace their notes.
The joy of laughter extends,
And everyone's shuffling coats.

When hot cocoa meets whipped cream,
It's a messy, sweet delight.
We raise our mugs, share a dream,
In this warmth, all feels right.

Heartstrings Intertwined

Two cats fight for the best seat,
One leaps high, misses the ledge.
The other snickers, quick on feet,
While the dog rolls off the hedge.

Grandma's cookies fill the air,
But Uncle Joe steals them with glee.
The kitchen's packed, a wondrous fair,
Where flour falls like a snowy spree.

Kids are mixing up their cheer,
Spilling sprinkles over the floor.
Their laughter ringing crystal clear,
As frosting gets stuck to the door.

In this chaos, hearts unite,
With all our funny little quirks.
Every moment feels so right,
In our web of joyous works.

The Breath of Winter's Cheer

Icicles hang like crystal tubes,
And penguins waddle in style.
Snowflakes cover the laughing cubes,
While snowball fights bring a smile.

Chubby cheeks, rosy and bright,
Kids tumble down snowy hills.
A hot pack here makes it right,
With cocoa for all the spills.

The ice rink's thrilled, and oh my,
As skaters wobble like ducks.
Spinning around, hear the sigh,
Of laughter, not just for lucks.

Winter's breath sings a tune,
Every moment, a silly dance.
Under stars, we'll croon and swoon,
At life's funny, bright romance.

Portraits of Tranquility

Cats in blankets, snug and tight,
Purring softly, oh so sweet.
While children dream of flying kites,
In a world of snow and heat.

Mugs of tea with a large splash,
Laughter bubbles, a friendly brawl.
Just beware of the biscuit crash,
Or be caught in a cookie thrall.

With each quirky mishap shared,
The warmth spreads through thick and thin.
Every goofy moment declared,
As our hearts all wear a grin.

In the cozy, laughter we find,
A peaceful bond, a joyful sight.
In these portraits of hearts entwined,
Winter's joy shines ever bright.

Threads of Connection

When penguins waddle in a line,
They giggle like they've had too much wine.
A snowman's carrot finds its way,
To join the dance on a sunny day.

Friends gather 'round with hats so bright,
They try to catch snowflakes in the night.
A snowball fight turns into glee,
While one slips back and lands in a tree.

Gifts wrapped in paper that's wrinkled and torn,
We laugh at the cat who's up on the horn.
Every crinkle and wrinkle just adds to the cheer,
As we unwrap the laughter that's waiting right here.

So come share a laugh, don't be so shy,
Join the frolic beneath the sky.
With a scoop of fun and a sprinkle of grace,
We'll wear our smiles like a warm embrace.

Affirmations of the Heart

The cookies burnt, but our spirits soar,
We laugh at the smoke that fills the door.
Gathered around with hearts so wide,
We toast with mugs, and let joy glide.

A cat in a hat steals the scene,
Chasing baubles like a festive queen.
The lights keep blinking in perfect array,
As we cheer each faultless display.

We dance by the tree, so jolly and plump,
With Aunt Edna's perfume, we all take a jump.
Every giggle and snort fills the air,
While we swap our stories without a care.

Under the stars, we toast to our flaws,
Shouting out loud, "We're all Santa's cause!"
With laughter and love, we brighten the night,
Affirming together that all will be right.

Embracing the Chill

Frosty nips at our noses bright,
While we sip cocoa by the firelight.
In dance-offs on ice, we go full flair,
As even the snowflakes seem to stare.

Nuts frozen solid, we try to crack,
With only our laughter to follow our hack.
A chilly breeze, yet spirits run hot,
We bundle up snug in a merry knot.

Sledding down hills with a squeal and a shout,
While a snowball fight turns into a rout.
Swaddled in scarves, we tumble and fall,
Finding pure joy in the laughter of all.

So here's to the cold, let's raise a cheer,
For making such memories year after year.
The chill in the air, we embrace with delight,
Knowing warmth comes from friends, in this frosty night.

Winter's Blissful Abode

In a cozy nook, we gather 'round,
With socks mismatched, our laughter astound.
The gingerbread house leans a bit too far,
As we munch on candy like it's a bazaar.

The fire pops and crackles, a toasty delight,
While grandpa tells tales that last through the night.
His stories are whacky, but we don't care,
We're too busy munching on popcorn to share.

Snowflakes are dancing; oh, what a sight,
As we trip on our skates, but it feels just right.
The snowman's nose might be slightly askew,
But in our hearts, it's the best view too.

So let's wrap up warm, with laughter and cheer,
In this blissful abode, let's keep drawing near.
With every warm hug and silly little jest,
Winter's our playground; we're truly blessed.

Candles in the Night

In the corner flickers light,
A cat's tail swishes, what a sight.
Spilled wax on grandma's chair,
A funny smell fills the air.

Laughter bounces off the walls,
Dance of shadows, laughter calls.
The dog sniffs where the candle was,
Confused about his latest fuzz.

Gingerbread men on the sill,
Each one sporting quite the thrill.
Icing on chips, who would have thought?
A wintry snack, joyfully sought.

Mismatched socks next to the fire,
An odd pair, one's pink, the other a flyer.
We giggle at our silly ways,
In this glow, our heart plays.

Essence of Home

There's a smell of burnt pies in the air,
Grandpa's jokes, a little rare.
Cookies mixed with cat's fine fur,
Laughter echoes with a gentle slur.

Slippers fluffy, not quite worn,
The pup cuddles, all but forlorn.
Coffee spills on Auntie's dress,
Yet somehow, it's all a success.

Children chase around the room,
In this chaos, feel the bloom.
A dance-off starts with a squeaky toy,
In every corner, there's a joy.

The tree's lopsided, lights askew,
Yet, this is home—so warm and true.
With every laugh and silly cheer,
We draw our loved ones ever near.

Fragments of Joy

A present wrapped with sneaky tape,
The cat leaps in with grand escape.
Ribbons flying, paper's torn,
In the chaos laughter's born.

Cookies stacked, one tipsy slide,
Down they tumble, oh, what a ride!
A race to catch the frosting's wail,
As Grandpa yells, "Let's not fail!"

Holiday lights flash and blink,
The dog chases, what a stink!
Frantic as a mouse in a trap,
We laugh outright, who needs a nap?

Mom holds up that sweater, bright,
"Who wore this? It's giving me fright!"
Yet amidst the laughs and silly ploys,
We find our fragments filled with joys.

The Dance of Warmth

The fire crackles with a sizzle,
A dance begins with a giggle and drizzle.
Grandma twirls in her fuzzy dress,
We join in, it's quite the mess.

With marshmallows stuck to our nose,
We prance around like silly crows.
Uncle plays tunes on a beat-up box,
While Auntie's face is covered in socks.

Outside the snow begins to fall,
Turning the world into a white ball.
We leap and pout in the frosty air,
Build a snowman with nary a care.

As laughter meets the glowing night,
Each moment's spark feels just right.
In our hearts, we feel it's true,
The warmth around is me and you.

Lanterns of Messenger Light

In the dark, a glow appears,
A cat knocked over all the beers.
We laugh at spills, we cheer the mess,
This festive night is quite the jest.

With lanterns hung from every tree,
A squirrel steals the cheese from me.
Lights flicker like a runaway mouse,
Who knew our home would be a house?

Eggnog spills and cookies fall,
A jolly laugh echoes through the hall.
This merry night, we sing and chime,
It's chaos, but it's also prime.

So raise a glass to goofy cheer,
We'll toast to all that brings us near.
With laughter loud and spirits bright,
Our hearts glow warm, our souls alight.

Springtime of the Soul

Spring has sprung with flowers bright,
But I tripped over my dog's delight.
With every sneeze, a giggle flows,
As pollen dances in the nose.

Bunnies hop without a care,
While I step softly in my chair.
Garden gnomes all stare and smirk,
Who knew they could be so jerky and quirk?

The sun smiles down on our parade,
But I'm still lost in last night's charade.
My dance moves? An awkward slide,
Reality's grip I cannot abide.

So let's embrace this springy cheer,
With petals flying, let's have no fear.
For life's a giggle wrapped in bloom,
We'll laugh our way right through the gloom.

Sweet Embrace of Togetherness

The group hug starts a little tight,
Someone sneezes, what a fright!
With bonds so strong, we squeeze out loud,
Yet all fall down, a tangled crowd.

Potluck table, food galore,
I brought a dish that none would explore.
Safe bets are cookies, but alas,
Mine looked like a mess — out of class!

We gather 'round with silly tales,
Of past mistakes and giant snails.
In laughter's grip, we can't outrun,
The joy mixed in with every pun.

So lift your glass, let love ignite,
Together's where we find our light.
In every gaffe, a heart does grow,
In sweet embrace, we steal the show.

Radiance of the Heart's Garden

In the garden, blooms arise,
Yet so do jokes and silly ties.
I water plants, my pants are wet,
The hose mischief, I'll never forget.

Butterflies dance without a clue,
While ants conspire to dance for two.
Roses blush at all our glee,
How did this mess come from me?

We dig for joy with every spade,
But weeds take over, plans get delayed.
With laughter strong, we pull and tug,
In every flower, there's a hug.

So let's embrace this garden's lore,
With laughter echoing forevermore.
For in this soil where humor grows,
The heart's true glow is what we chose.

Comfort's Embrace

In a chair that squeaks quite loud,
I snuggle with my cozy shroud.
My cat's on my lap, snoring with glee,
While I sip hot cocoa—oh, so heavenly!

The dog is trying to steal my treat,
A chocolate bar, oh what a feat!
But I can't help but laugh out loud,
This chaos is a comfort crowd!

The sock war rages on the floor,
How did I lose ten socks or more?
But no worries echo through the air,
In this mess, I find joy everywhere!

So here's to life's silly little charms,
Wrapped in laughter, cuddles, and alarms.
Let the world dance in hiccuping delight,
Finding joy in nonsense, day and night.

The Gift of Hope

A gift-wrapped pickle sits under the tree,
Surprising my brother, oh what glee!
He opens it slow, a frown and then grin,
This is the weirdest holiday win!

A sweater that shrunk from extra heat,
I slip it on, feeling like a treat.
My shoulder's now dressed in a woolly bowl,
Yet still I prance with a jolly soul.

In the card, I wrote with a twist of fate,
"Happy new year, here's a cheese plate!"
With sausage and crackers, oh such a sight,
We celebrate laughter, that feels so right.

Hope springs from silliness, brightening our ways,
In giggles and chuckles, we spend our days.
So pass me the pickles, I'll share my cheer,
With family and friends, let's toast with a beer!

Enchanted Evening Dreams

The moon winks playfully down on my bed,
With dreams of chocolate dancing in my head.
I reach for a cookie—oops, it's a shoe!
But who needs proper when dessert will do?

A blanket fort whispers, "Come have some fun!"
With pillows that giggle, we're never done.
As we tell ghost stories, the shadows all flip,
And laugh at the monsters that out of my grip.

A marshmallow war breaks out like a show,
Sticky delights flying fast like a bow.
Amid all the chaos, joy starts to gleam,
In our enchanted evening, we soar and we dream.

The stars start to twinkle, embracing our cheers,
In this jumbled haven, we're free from our fears.
With laughter as magic filling the room,
We sleep in delight, sweet dreams will bloom.

Journey Through the Hearth

An oven mitt laughs, a spatula sings,
As I fumble with flour and all of its flings.
Baking my troubles into muffins so sweet,
Only to find that I burned the whole treat!

The dog jumps up, trying to snag a bite,
While I dance in the kitchen, feeling quite bright.
Flour on my nose, a whisk in my hand,
In this joyful mess, life's perfectly planned.

The cookies are lopsided, a hodgepodge of cheer,
I dish them out freely, "Hey, come grab your share!"
With laughter and crumbs covering the floor,
Every mistake is worth more than before.

So here's to mishaps and giggles galore,
The heart of the kitchen, forever we'll adore.
In the warmth of this chaos, we all find our place,
Sharing joy through our laughter and cookie embrace.

Joyful Echoes of the Heart

When laughter rains like cat and dog,
A jolly dance begins, no need to hog.
With silly hats and socks askew,
Joy erupts in every view.

A tickle here, a giggle there,
We toss all worries, float in air.
From clumsy moves to banana peels,
Our hearts burst forth with joy that heals.

The punchline lands, we're rolling 'round,
In fits of glee, we've truly found.
Those moments bright, like candy bright,
In joyful echoes, we take flight.

So let's embrace our quirks and charms,
With open hearts, we'll spill our arms.
For in the laughter, love will spark,
As joy ignites, it lights the dark.

Glimpses of a Better Tomorrow

On cloudy days, we find the sun,
With mismatched socks, we laugh and run.
A silly dance in grocery aisles,
Each frozen smile brings out the wiles.

Tomorrow's plans with a twist of fate,
We'll fry the wrongs, and celebrate.
With burnt toast crunched and coffee spills,
We laugh at our delightful thrills.

Picturesque dreams with rainbows bright,
In our spaghetti fights, we feel so light.
With friends beside and laughter loud,
We twirl our dreams in every crowd.

So here's to fun, let worries flee,
With gleeful hearts, we're wild and free.
In every mishap, we'll cheer out loud,
For better days are our proud shroud.

Wings of Reassurance

When life gets tough, just grab a laugh,
Don't take the road, just take the path.
In wobbly steps, we find our grace,
With silly faces, we smile with pace.

A flock of ducks in a silly line,
Quacking loudly, they've crossed the sign.
With flapping arms and goofy glee,
We soar above, like birds so free.

When troubles poke like sharpest pricks,
Just crack a joke and throw some tricks.
In fluffy clouds, we chase our dreams,
With laughter high, or so it seems.

So join the flight, spread out your wings,
In foolish fun, we're kings and queens.
Through all the chuckles, love will thrive,
With laughter's glow, we're so alive.

The Calm Amidst the Storm

When raindrops dance and wind does howl,
We find our peace, like wise old owl.
With cozy socks and hugs so tight,
We weather storms with sheer delight.

In popcorn fights and movie screens,
We make our dreams from whipped-up schemes.
With quirky jokes and witticism,
We paint the dark in jest's prism.

Under blankets snuggled warm and tight,
As chaos swirls, we glow with light.
It's in the giggles that we find,
A calming balm for troubled mind.

So when it storms, don't hide away,
Just pull up chairs and laugh today.
For in the chaos that might loom,
We'll find the magic in every room.

Kindling Spirits

When the firewood's stacked so high,
We pretend it's a pie in the sky.
Grandma's cooking makes us all cheer,
Until we find her 'secret' is beer.

Stockings hung with care and flair,
One's a sock, we know it's rare.
The cat's now tangled in the lights,
While we debate our tree's strange heights.

Laughter spills like cocoa cups,
As Dad pretends to fix things up.
Mom's burning cookies in the back,
Yet all we taste is her sweet smack.

So gather 'round and laugh aloud,
This goofy bunch, we're still so proud.
With mishaps that we all adore,
This merry mess? Who could want more!

Footprints in the Snow

Out in the snow, we make our prints,
Like clumsy ducks, we dare to squint.
Falling down, we can't help but laugh,
Our pants get soaked—this isn't a bath!

Snowballs fly like wild, lost dreams,
As we plot mischief with our schemes.
The neighbors glare with frostbit eyes,
While we giggle like we're the wise.

Cocoa spills from a wobbly mug,
As we blame the dog—it's quite the shrug.
Sipping warmth on a frosty eve,
Yet all that's left—sorry, we cleave!

So cheer we must, as snowflakes sway,
In this winter wonderland play.
With laughter echoing through the glow,
These silly messes help love grow!

Emblems of Affection

Cards are sent with hearts so bright,
Yet they always look a tad slight.
Grandpa's jokes inside each one,
Make us roll our eyes, oh, what fun!

Wrapped up gifts that don't quite fit,
Unraveled chaos, here we sit.
Layered hugs and mismatched socks,
Comical thoughts from even rocks.

Cookies shaped like grandma's face,
We munch and giggle, oh, what grace!
Frosting's spilled on the table too,
"Happy accidents," Grandpa knew.

Together here with love à la mode,
Making memories on this road.
So here's a toast with joyful cheer,
To the funny bonds we hold dear!

Embracing Every Tear

When the fridge runs low on cheer,
And the turkey's lost, that's clear.
A dance with flour, just off beat,
As we churn our giggles, can't be beat.

Tears of laughter, we often share,
With smudged makeup and tousled hair.
Mom's in a frenzy, it's all a show,
While we play rescue, full of woe.

Messy meals on the table spread,
As the dog burps, we all turn red.
But amid the chaos, warmth remains,
In every smile, and in our games.

So raise a glass to what we keep,
These joyful follies run so deep.
In every tear, a spark we find,
It's the laughter that's truly kind.

Echoes of Happiness

When the cat steals your chair, oh what a sight,
As you balance on cushions, holding on tight.
Laughter erupts at the dog's silly dance,
In this home filled with joy, we take every chance.

The fridge is a treasure, or so it may seem,
With leftovers hidden like a long-lost dream.
The cake that was made, now just crumbs on a plate,
Brings smiles to our faces, it's never too late.

Our socks are mismatched, just add to the fun,
While we race to the couch, it's a chaotic run.
Joy comes in moments, not always just planned,
Like a pie that is cooling, right under your hand.

So raise up your glass, to dear friends by our side,
In laughter and chaos, let humor be our guide.
Life's little mischiefs, keep hearts ever light,
As we dance in the kitchen, till the end of the night.

Radiance in the Shadows

In the corner, the dog's snoring like a bear,
While the cat claims the sun with a raised, fluffy flare.
The shadows just giggle, secrets they keep,
As we dream of the cookies that never see sleep.

With a wink and a nod, through the bustle we glide,
In puddles of laughter, we gladly abide.
The mysteries grow loud; come join in the spree,
Chasing echoes of joy, echoing merrily.

We stumble on toys, our quest ever dire,
As the kids build a castle, with few rights to aspire.
The remote's gone missing; it's lost in the fray,
Yet we find in our chaos a new game to play.

So toast to the mishaps, the laughter we bring,
In shadows and light, our hearts always sing.
Life's silliness glimmers, as night softly falls,
In the warmth of our home, true joy never stalls.

Sparkles of Serenity

A squirrel in the yard seems quite full of glee,
As he plots for the nuts, that are intended for me.
With a wink at the chaos, the sun shines so bright,
It's a party of laughter, from morning till night.

The kettle's a-blur, on its own little quest,
With steam rising up, it's time for a jest.
The coffee spills over, the laughter erupts,
As the toast burns to char, we all just erupt.

The plants in the window, dance to the tune,
A jive of the leaves, with a love for the moon.
Worms wiggle in soil, and they giggle with cheer,
For every small hiccup, brings comfort so near.

So let's scoop up the giggles, and sprinkle them wide,
In the simplest moments, we find joy inside.
May every small sparkle bring warmth to our hearts,
As we laugh through the days, from the cares we depart.

Melodies of Solace

Oh, the symphony's led by a sneaky old goat,
Who's stealing the carrots, the best he can tote.
Each note is a chuckle, each rest, a delight,
As we sway to the rhythm of our odd little night.

With the cat on the piano, imagine the tune,
While the parrot's off-key sings 'La la' by noon.
The splat of some paint, from our artful despair,
Turns the walls into stories, with giggles to spare.

A roast in the oven is now quite a fright,
As it dances and twirls in a comedic flight.
While we gather around, with our forks all in hand,
The fun's in the feast, not just what we planned.

So here's to the laughter, and joy that we share,
In the winks, and the mishaps, savor every glare.
Life is a melody, with harmony sweet,
As we prance through the chaos, on our own little beat.

Sparks of Joyful Remembrance

In December's chill, we wear socks so bright,
With patterns of snowmen, a truly odd sight.
We dance around, like penguins on ice,
Spilling hot cocoa, oh, isn't it nice?

Grandma's fruitcake still makes us all laugh,
We joke it's a weapon, just check the staff!
Each slice a mystery, a taste to explore,
Swapping our bites, we can't take anymore!

A cactus as a gift? It's somewhat bizarre,
Yet Uncle Joe hugs it, he'll drive it real far.
Advent calendars with jokes make us cheer,
Each chocolate reveals such odd tales of the year!

So let's raise a cup, with marshmallows piled high,
To the joys of these moments, as time flutters by.
We'll cherish the laughter, and the mishaps we find,
Creating new memories, a patchwork of mind!

The Language of Kindred Spirits

We gather each year, with stories to share,
In mismatched pajamas, we form quite a pair.
My brother spills eggnog, it's sticky and sweet,
He slips on the carpet, now that's quite a feat!

The cat steals our snacks, he reigns like a king,
As laughter erupts from the chaos he brings.
We swap silly tales of that one awkward dance,
And how Auntie's fruit punch put us in a trance!

The roast was a flop, a disaster divine,
But who can resist that old bottle of wine?
We toast to the blunders, the smiles they've unfurled,
In this language of joy, we share with the world!

With each crazy story, our spirits ignite,
Connecting with laughter, our hearts feel so light.
Kindred in chaos, we sing through the night,
Creating our language, a bond that feels right!

A Quilt of Golden Memories

Wrapped in our blankets, we gather around,
With grandma's old quilt, we're forever bound.
It's stitched with our laughs and a few silly frowns,
A patchwork of moments, no room for the downs.

Each square tells a tale, some sweeter than pie,
Like cousin Lou's antics, oh my, oh my!
We recount the time he wore socks on his hands,
Getting lost in the woods while searching for cans!

Then there's Aunt Patty, with cookies galore,
She mixed up her spices; we still ask for more.
Each bite is an adventure, a playful delight,
That keeps all our spirits shining so bright!

So let's sew a new patch, with laughter and cheer,
Into this warm quilt, our memories dear.
With every small stitch, we weave love so tight,
In our quilt of gold, joy glimmers at night!

Serenity's Soft Caress

On a chilly night, with hot tea in hand,
We snuggle together, the happiest band.
Oh! Somebody's snoring—who could it be?
The dog's in a dreamland, quite happy, you see.

The fairy lights twinkle, with a glow that's so bright,
As we doodle our wishes till late in the night.
Mom's making soup, an aromatic tease,
While dad's searching for new ways to sneeze!

We draft playful poems, just silly and fun,
About Uncle Bob's wig, oh where has it run?
Soft laughter tumbles like snowflakes in air,
As we wrap joy in friendship, a love we all share.

With mugs overflowing, this calmness is bliss,
Serenity's touch in each laugh and each kiss.
So let's raise our voices, loud and sincere,
To the warmth of our hearts, a melody dear!

A Promise in the Silence

In the quiet of the night, a sneeze,
A distant jingle, what could it be?
Santa's reindeer, or a cat on a spree,
Dancing on rooftops, mischievous and free.

The cookies left out, they seem to have grown,
A bite so big, it's clearly not bone!
Maybe a bear found the snack zone,
Or just Uncle Joe, who thinks he's alone.

With a giggle and cheer, we light up the room,
Grandma's scarf matches the cat's big bloom.
The festive season, a colorful boom,
With laughter and love, we're blooming in gloom.

So raise up a glass, to the fun that we make,
To bloopers and giggles, and the joy that we bake.
These moments of chaos, they're ours for the take,
In the silence of laughter, we wake from the fake.

Shadows of Serenity

In the shadows we hide, just a game of charades,
Dressed as holiday cheer, in mismatched parades.
While Grandma is snoring, the adults have strayed,
In the depth of our laughter, mischief cascades.

The fruitcake lies dormant, a science project,
No one will eat it, what a bizarre reject!
A doorbell rings loud, what a surprise effect,
It's our neighbor, he's here to inspect!

The lights start to twinkle, a dance in the night,
Glittering chaos, a chandelier fright.
We play hide-and-seek with the holiday light,
Giggling loudly, it's a hilarious sight.

So raise your glasses, for laughter that's sweet,
Let's toast to this life, where odd is the beat.
Joy found in shadows, where we are discreet,
In this comedy dance, we can't help but tweet!

The Light in Our Eyes

With twinkles of mischief, the lights we adore,
A squirrel stole the star, oh what a score!
Hanging high on the roof, it wanted much more,
Now it darts through the trees, what a festive folklore!

Grandpa's old sweater has a story to tell,
With reindeer, and snowflakes, and the faint scent of gel.
He claims he's a model, though we can't quite quell,
The laughter and snorts that so readily swell.

In this colorful chaos, we share all the quirks,
A punch bowl of giggles, joyful jerks.
The cats climb the tree, oh the mayhem it lurks,
Dancing alongside, while the puppy just perks.

So here's to the season, with memories bright,
Where humor ignites our festive delight.
With every silly tale, and every goodnight,
We gather together, our hearts taking flight.

Mosaic of Togetherness

In the mosaic we create, a patchwork of cheer,
Each tile has a story, and some, oh dear!
From Auntie's wild dance to the dog's joyful beer,
Together we laugh, it's our holiday sphere.

The kitchen is buzzing, oh my, what a smell!
A disaster afoot, you can instantly tell.
From the burnt, crispy edges, our fate does compel,
We toast to the mishaps, while ringing the bell.

With every moment shared, our hearts grow in size,
Fleeting little echoes, where each giggle flies.
In the warmth of our gatherings, the laughter applies,
Mosaic of joy, beneath chilly blue skies.

So gather around, as we reminisce funny,
With stories so bright, like the sun or the honey.
We'll cherish these memories, each one but a bunny,
In the tapestry of love, we spark laughter sunny.

Milton Keynes UK
Ingram Content Group UK Ltd.
UKHW021242191124
451300UK00007B/191